Gymnastics

Rita Storey

FRANKLIN WATTS
LONDON • SYDNEY

First published in 2010 by
Franklin Watts
338 Euston Road
London NW1 3BH

Franklin Watts Australia
Level 17/207 Kent Street
Sydney NSW 2000

Words in **bold** are in the glossary on page 30.

Series editor: Julia Bird
Art director: Jonathan Hair

Series designed and created for Franklin Watts by Storeybooks.
Designer: Rita Storey
Editor: Nicola Barber
Photography: Tudor Photography, Banbury (unless otherwise stated)

Picture credits
Richard Heathcote/Getty Images pp 26 and 29; i-stock pp 6 and 24.

Thanks to Pinewood Gymnastics Club, Edgbarrow Trampoline Club and Woking
Gymnastics Club. Also thanks to Beth Andrew, Miki Chu, Lucie Colebeck and Sophie
Lewis for their participation in the book.

A CIP catalogue record for this book is available from the British Library.

Dewey classification: 796.4'42
ISBN: 978 0 7496 9538 5

Printed in China

Franklin Watts is a division of Hachette
Children's Books, an Hachette UK company.
www.hachette.co.uk

Contents

Meet the gymnasts

There are several different types of gymnastics. Each type uses different skills, but all of them require a combination of flexibility, strength, co-ordination, balance, elegance and bravery.

Types of gymnastics

Artistic gymnastics and trampolining are both Olympic sports for men and women. Rhythmic gymnastics is also an Olympic sport for women. To perform well in any type of gymnastics requires a great deal of training and dedication.

In this book you will meet four gymnasts who will share their experiences with you, and show you what it takes to be a gymnast performing at the highest level.

Types of gymnastics

Men and women

Artistic Performed using six pieces of **apparatus** for men, four for women. Individuals and teams compete (see pages 14–17).

Trampolining – Individual Routines made up of ten moves performed on a trampoline. Individuals and teams compete. – **Synchronised** Pairs of trampolinists perform the same routines side-by-side on two trampolines. – **Double mini-trampoline** Routines performed on specially designed trampolines with two separate parts (see pages 18–19).

Tumbling A series of spectacular somersaults and twists performed on a 25 m track. Individuals and teams compete (see pages 20–21).

Aerobic Routines that include jumps and leaps, performed to lively music in twos, threes and teams of six.

Acrobatic Routines that use complicated acrobatic moves, performed to music. Pairs, fours and mixed pairs compete.

Women

Rhythmic Routines using five pieces of apparatus – ball, ribbon, hoop, clubs and rope.

Beth Andrew

I am 14 years old and I am an artistic gymnast. I came 19th in the English Championships in 2009. In the same year I also won a silver individual medal and a gold team medal at the Grade 1 National Finals, and a gold medal at the Southern Region Challenge Cup.

As well as gymnastics, I love reading, baking and scrapbooking. My favourite subjects at school are History, Latin and Greek.

Miki Chu

I am 12 years old and I am an artistic gymnast. As well as gymnastics, I like break-dancing, cars and robots.

My main achievement so far is a silver medal at the South East Regional Finals in 2009. I finished 21st out of the 60 best Under-12 gymnasts in Great Britain.

Sophie Lewis

I am 15 years old and I am a trampolinist. I am the Welsh Open female National Champion and I have won junior championships in Portugal (2007, 2008 and 2009) and in the Czech Republic (2009). In 2009 I also represented Great Britain in the World Age Group Championships in Russia. I came 39th, so I am now 39th in the world in the 15–16 age group.

As well as trampolining, I like listening to music and swimming.

Lucie Colebeck

I am 13 years old and I am a tumbler. I was British Champion in my age group in 2008 and 2009. I won championships in Portugal (2008), Ireland (2009) and Belgium (2009). In 2009 I represented GB (Great Britain) in the 13–14 years World Age Group Championships in Russia. I also won two gold medals at the British Tumbling Tournament.

As well as gymnastics, I love all sorts of other sports.

Starting out

Gymnastics is one of the most popular sports in Great Britain, with an estimated four million people taking part. As well as being an elite sport, gymnastics is a fun hobby for people of all ages.

Gymnastics for everyone

There are gym clubs in towns, villages and schools everywhere where young people can get their first taste of gymnastics.

Little children love to run and jump. Gym clubs run kindergyms and toddler classes for children from a few months old. These classes are designed to be great fun. They also help little children to gain confidence with their balance and co-ordination. As they get older, children begin to learn a greater range of skills.

As they reach school age, children may start to go to **recreational** gym classes. Clubs often run their own progress schemes in gymnastics. Those who go to classes can earn badges and certificates as they learn new skills and move on to new levels.

As they get older, some young gymnasts may decide to specialise in different styles of gymnastics. Some will join **TeamGym**, where they work as part of a team to perform floor, **trampette** and tumbling programmes to music. Others may prefer trampolining, tumbling or

My mum took me along to the local gym club when I was just two-and-a-half years old.

I started recreational gymnastics when I was four and moved on to TeamGym with my older sister. When I was nine, the coach at the club asked me if I wanted to do artistic gymnastics and said that they would fast track me. I was really excited.

Some very small children have no problems with flexibility!

rhythmic gymnastics. Those gymnasts who want to specialise in artistic gymnastics will begin to use apparatus such as the vault and balance beams (see pages 14–17). The choice may depend on what is on offer in the area, as gym clubs do not always run classes in every type of gymnastics.

Going further

For many young people, doing classes at their local gym club and getting badges will be enough. Other gymnasts who show promise may be chosen to represent their clubs in competitions. Competition squads train more regularly. They compete against other clubs and at county, regional and national levels against others in their age group.

Those with the talent and dedication to go even further may be chosen to attend trials. They may have the opportunity to compete for their home nation, or for Great Britain at European and World championships.

I started gymnastics when I was nine years old. I just tried it to see if I would like it. I saw all the other tumblers doing back flips and I wanted to do the same.

Mum took me to a recreational gymnastics class when I was four because she needed to wear me out – I was a lousy sleeper! I had my first trampoline class when I was eight and moved to Edgbarrow Trampoline Club when I was nine to do competitive trampolining.

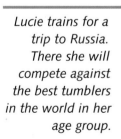

Lucie trains for a trip to Russia. There she will compete against the best tumblers in the world in her age group.

Coach's notes: starting young

To stand a chance of reaching the level of flexibility required to compete at a high level, boys have to start gymnastics very young. Girls seem to be more naturally flexible and can catch up if they start later.

In training

Gymnasts must train regularly to perform at their best. They must be strong, fit and very flexible. Their training includes a range of different exercises to strengthen their muscles and bring their bodies up to a high level of general fitness and flexibility.

Warm up

Before they begin a training session, gymnasts warm up their muscles with a series of exercises done on the move. This is called a **cardiovascular** warm up. These exercises are designed to increase the heart rate and strengthen the heart and lungs. Jogging around the mat is a simple cardiovascular exercise.

Stretches done on the move, called **dynamic stretches**, are the second type of exercise. Leg swings at the ballet barre are an example of a dynamic stretching exercise.

*We start our **warm up** by jogging around the mat a few times to get the blood pumping!*

Lucie and Beth warm up before a training session.

Lucie prepares for an energetic training session by doing dynamic stretches.

I train five times a week for between two-and-a-half and three hours. There isn't any part of my training that I don't enjoy!

Trampoline warm up

Trampolinists can get straight on to the trampoline to do their warm up. Gentle trampolining is very good cardiovascular exercise, and stretching while bouncing is a good way of doing dynamic stretches.

Stretching

When they are warmed up, the gymnasts begin a series of exercises to stretch every muscle group in their body. This routine is very important as it prepares the muscles for the practice session and helps to prevent muscle damage.

Sophie does her dynamic stretches on the trampoline.

*I train for 22.5 hours a week:
Tuesday – 7am to 9.30am and 5pm to 8pm.
Wednesday, Thursday and Friday – 5pm to 8pm.
Saturday – 2pm to 6pm.
Sunday – 10am to 2pm.*

Lucie must warm up and stretch every part of her body. Even her wrists (right) and ankles (top) are flexed before she starts her routine.

Core strength

There are more than 30 separate muscles across the back, stomach and hips. These are known as the **core muscles**. Exercising and strengthening these muscles gives a gymnast a solid foundation of strength and fitness, and helps to prevent injury.

Trampolinists do their core fitness training after training sessions on the trampoline.

I train six days a week. Most of the sessions are two hours long – one-and-a-half hours on the trampoline and half an hour of **conditioning** *afterwards. For one session, I spend two hours on the trampoline. As well as trampoline training, I try to get down to the local pool to swim as often as I can.*

Sophie does the exercise shown in the pictures (left and below left) to strengthen her core muscles.

Rope climbing helps to develop upper body strength.

Power

Gymnasts need power in their legs to propel themselves upwards to perform somersaults and flips. Their training includes specific exercises to strengthen the upper body and legs.

Plyometrics

Plyometrics are exercises designed to help muscles to stretch and then **contract**. The aim of plyometrics is to improve muscle power. These exercises are used by elite athletes in lots of different sports.

I train for over 20 hours a week, including six hours every Saturday. I do an energetic warm up every day, as well as strength and flexibility exercises. I prefer learning new skills to the rest of the training.

In this plyometric exercise Miki's coach helps Miki to increase his muscle power.

Flexibility

Flexibility is vital to a gymnast. As gymnasts perform their routines they push their bodies to reach and bend to the maximum. In order to do this without injuring themselves, they must follow a strict training programme that improves their flexibility gradually, over a long period of time.

Miki must train hard to develop his flexibility.

Cool down

At the end of a session, gymnasts do another series of stretches to cool down. These **static stretches** are held for a longer time than the dynamic stretches, and are done while the player is still. Static stretches allow the muscles to relax and prevent them from stiffening up and causing **cramp**.

*As well as the warm up and conditioning training, a session for tumblers includes things like handstands on to a **springboard**, back flips and a row of **whips**. My favourite part is on the **tumble track**. (See pages 20–21 for more about tumbling.)*

The role of the coach

A coach plays an important part in the life of an elite gymnast for many years. A coach is there for training sessions, and he or she travels to all the competitions with the gymnasts as well.

The role of the coach

It is the coach's job to design the gymnast's training programme so that he or she reaches maximum potential at just the right moment. To do this, a coach monitors every aspect of a gymnast's performance and develops a training programme designed to increase fitness and improve technique.

Performance analysis

Watching playbacks on laptops or even on a mobile phone can help to identify problems or highlight achievements in a gymnast's routine.

A trampolining coach sometimes uses a stopwatch to time ten jumps, then thirty jumps. These timings can be compared every few weeks to work out how high the gymnast is jumping.

A mobile phone can be used to film routines and play them back instantly. This can be very useful in a training session.

I have one main coach, Sue Lawton. She's trained Olympic athletes and is an amazing coach. I also have Nick who helps me when I'm learning new moves, Jess who is great for conditioning training, and Pip who advises me.

Sue specialises in psychology. She has taught me how to think through each routine before I start performing it in a competition.

I have one main coach – Simon Elliott. I have other coaches, too, who help me with different parts of my training.

Motivation

Good coaches know all their gymnasts well and understand how to get the best out of each one. Some gymnasts like to be challenged with set targets; others prefer competing against others. Some gymnasts enjoy improving their own performance but get very nervous in competitions. It is up to the coach to identify these traits and to work with each gymnast to find a way of achieving the best possible performance.

Coaches are on hand to congratulate their gymnasts when they win, and support them when they lose. They are often former elite performers themselves, and can understand how the gymnast is feeling.

Coaches need to motivate their gymnasts when training is hard.

Simon supports Miki as he tries out a new part of his routine on the parallel bars.

My coach is called Vladimir Podobin. He has helped many of us to get to the World Age Group Championships. He has been chosen to come to the Championships with us as coach.

Artistic gymnastics

Artistic gymnastics is the most popular type of gymnastics. Women perform on four pieces of apparatus, men on six. Women's routines are on the vault, asymmetric bars, **beam and floor. The men also perform on the vault and the floor, as well as the** pommel horse, rings, parallel bars **and** high bar.

Vault

The gymnast makes a fast run up to a springboard and then over a vaulting platform, while doing twists and somersaults. The routine is marked on technical difficulty as well as control of the vault and landing.

Asymmetric bars

This women's exercise includes continuous swinging movements in both directions, above and below the bars. It should contain twists and somersaults. A spectacular **dismount** often ends the routine.

Perfect score

The top score in gymnastics – a perfect 10.0 – was first achieved in the 1976 Olympic Games by the Romanian gymnast Nadia Comaneci. She went on to score six more 10.0s and win three gold medals. In 2006 the system of awarding points in gymnastics competitions was changed. In the new system there is no limit to the score a gymnast can be awarded. Points for the difficulty of the routine and the way it is performed are added together to make the final score.

Beth prepares to leap from the low to the high bar in her asymmetric bars routine.

Beth performs a **walkover** *as part of her* **balance beam** *routine.*

Balance beam

Women gymnasts perform a combination of acrobatic elements on a beam five metres long and ten centimetres wide. The gymnast uses great control and balance to do leaps and jumps while standing, sitting and lying on the beam. She must use the full length of the beam. The finish of the routine is a dismount that often contains spectacular acrobatic elements.

Women's floor

The women's floor exercise is a combination of dance and acrobatic moves. The routine can be up to 90 seconds long, and is performed to music. The **choreography** of the routine is extremely important. It should use the whole floor and be original and artistic, as well as technically challenging.

The floor exercise contains somersaults and twists.

Men's floor

The men's floor exercise takes between 50 and 70 seconds. The whole floor area must be used to perform a routine containing somersaults, twists and leaps.

Pommel horse

The pommel horse routine is a smooth, continuous series of moves, using all parts of the pommel horse (see below left). This routine needs great strength in the arms and upper body.

Rings

The gymnast performs this routine while hanging from two rings suspended on wire cables. During the routine the rings should stay still while the gymnast does a series of swings and static strength moves.

Vault

Like the women, the men gymnasts use a springboard to launch themselves over the vaulting platform while doing twists and somersaults.

A soft landing
The floor on which gymnasts perform contains springs and rubber to make it soft to land on. It is bouncy to give height to the gymnasts' routines.

Miki practises his floor routine.

Miki needs to have very strong arms and core muscles to do moves like this on the pommel horse.

Miki in action on the rings.

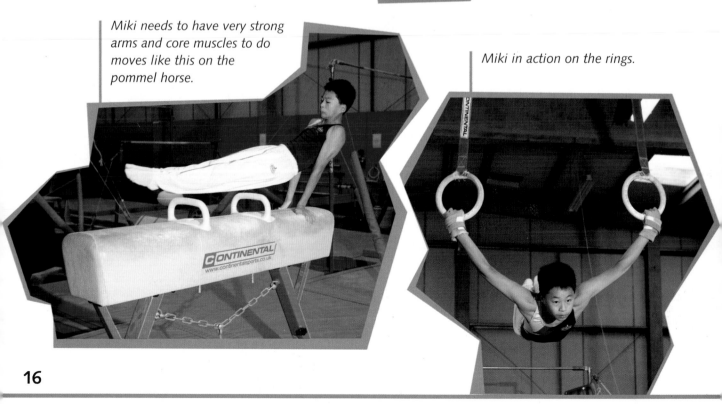

16

High bar

The gymnast performs continuous swinging movements around the bar. As the gymnast swings forwards and backwards he releases and re-grasps the bar. He must not touch the bar with his body. At the end of the routine, the dismount may include somersaults and twists.

Parallel bars

On the parallel bars the gymnast performs swinging movements and strength holds. The gymnast should work above, below and along the whole length of the bars.

Dismount

The finish is an important part of a routine for both men and women. The routines on the asymmetric bars, balance beam, pommel horse, rings, vault, parallel bars and high bar all end with a dismount. Marks are deducted for poor landings.

Miki keeps his body very straight as he swings round the high bar.

In this strength move on the parallel bars Miki holds a position perfectly still.

My least favourite events are the vault and the floor because my leg stamina is weak.

A perfect landing is one where the gymnast lands with his or her feet together and does not stumble or take a step.

Trampolining

Trampolining is great fun and very good exercise. Many young people have their first taste of trampolining in a garden. If they want to learn how to trampoline properly, they can join a club.

Trampolining is one of the newest Olympic sports. Elite trampolinists carry out spectacular routines containing jumps, somersaults and twists. To do this they can bounce to heights of up to six metres.

Many trampolinists who go to clubs are mainly interested in having fun and staying fit. But for those who wish to push themselves further, there are nine levels to progress through, from beginner to international. To qualify for each level you have to get the required number of points or a specific score in a competition.

Trials take place to select trampolinists with real potential to join elite training programmes.

In the top levels you can be moved down if you don't meet the requirements of the level you're in twice in a row. It's harsh, especially if you're working on a new routine. In artistic you can just get back on the apparatus if you fall off, but in trampolining if you make a wrong move, that's it – it's ruthless!

High flying

The first trampoline was constructed some time around 1934 by George Nissen and Larry Griswold at the University of Iowa. Early trampolines were developed as a training tool to be used by divers and skiers, as well as gymnasts. They were also used to train astronauts.

*Sophie does a three-quarter front somersault (left) and a double somersault in a **piked** position (right – see page 19).*

Sophie performs her routine at the 2009 National Trampoline Championships.

The moves

Jumps These can be done in a **tuck** position (knees to chest), a **straddle** position (legs out to the side, hands touching toes), or a pike position (legs out straight in front).

Twists These are also called rotations and can be done either to the right or the left, but must always be done the same way.

Landings These can be to seat (a sitting position), front or back.

Somersaults These can be done forwards or backwards. They can also be tucked, piked, straight or with a twist.

All these basic shapes are combined to make complex routines.

Competitions

In competitions a routine is made up from ten moves. There are three rounds in a competition. One round is a routine made up of **compulsory** elements. For top-level competitions these elements are set by the governing body for trampoline gymnastics, the *Federation Internationale de Gymnastique (FIG)*. Extra points are awarded for the degree of difficulty. The performers with the highest scores may compete in a second and third round.

Side-by-side

Synchronised trampolining is when two trampolinists perform the same routine side-by-side on two trampolines. They perform exactly the same moves in unison. They are marked individually and then points are added for the precision of their synchronisation.

Sophie and her partner compete in a National Sychronised Trampoline gala.

Tumbling

Lucie performs a high full twist as part of her routine.

Tumbling is performed by male and female gymnasts, both individually and as teams. Tumblers run along a 25-metre track before performing a series of spectacular twists and somersaults. A sequence takes only a few seconds, but the expertise needed to perfect such routines takes years of training and practice.

The special track on which tumblers perform their routines (**passes**) is soft and bouncy. This helps to protect the tumblers from injury and also gives them extra height for twists and somersaults.

In a competition, each gymnast performs two different passes (three if they make the final), each one containing eight skills. Each pass finishes with a dismount.

Go for gold

Tumbling was included in the Olympic Games for just one year in Los Angeles, 1932.

Tumbling became very popular in the 1960s and '70s in eastern Europe, and its popularity has now spread to the rest of the world.

The Trampoline and Tumbling World Championships include competitors from over 400 countries.

Some tumbling skills

Back handspring A move where the gymnast takes off from either one foot or both feet, jumps backwards on to the hands, then lands on the feet.

Salto (also called a flip or somersault) For this move the gymnast takes off, rotates horizontally, then lands back on the feet. It can be done with a tuck (knees to chest), a pike (legs out straight in front) or a layout (straight body position).

Round-off Similar to a cartwheel, but with both feet landing at the same time.

Whip A back flip done very fast with the body straight.

Top-class tumblers include two or sometimes three double somersaults in one pass, combined with twisting elements as well.

There are some similarities between tumbling and trampolining skills, and competitions for both are often held together.

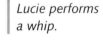

Lucie performs a whip.

A back handspring (left) and a round-off (right).

In competition

The years of training and preparation are put to the test when gymnasts take part in competitions.

Women artistic gymnasts usually perform in top-level competitions such as the World Championships or Olympic Games in their late teens. Male artistic gymnasts mostly peak later, in their late teens and early twenties.

Top-level trampolinists tend to be older than artistic gymnasts. Trampolinists in their thirties regularly compete in major competitions.

I have a plan on my calendar which starts with parts of routines, then half routines, building up to full routines before a competition.

On the day of a competition I warm up as normal, making sure I gently stretch every muscle. I go through the routine in my head, but apart from that I just try to do what I do in the gym every day.

We are preparing all season, but we put the routine together about three weeks before a competition. I decrease my training a few days before I compete.

On the day of a competition I eat a bigger breakfast, as I don't normally eat during the competition.

There isn't a dressing room – you are out on the floor – so the audience can see you prepare.

I've done so many competitions that I've learnt to deal with my nerves. I'm not very sociable before I compete. I listen to my iPod and get myself into my 'zone'.

Miki prepares his hands with special guards and chalk (for grip) to begin a routine on the parallel bars.

Being prepared

The preparation for a competition is both physical and mental. Although gymnasts may be competing as part of a team, each individual has to perform in front of a panel of judges. Conquering nerves can be the key to success for some gymnasts.

Three weeks before a competition I start to do practice competitions and routines every day.

On the day of the competition I warm up for ten minutes and then do some stretches.

Everyone gets nervous before they compete. I do deep breathing and mentally rehearse the routine to focus before I perform.

Before big competitions our coach conditions us much harder. We have to weigh ourselves and be careful about what we eat. We do more runs on the track every day. The morning of a competition is very nerve-racking. The warm up is the same as usual. Before I compete, I always listen to my coach.

When I compete, the adrenalin is overwhelming. It makes me determined to win.

Coach's notes: success

Male gymnasts start training when they are two or three years old. They will not get to the standard needed to compete in the Olympics until they are well into their twenties. Winning a gold medal may be down to a routine that is one-and-a-half minutes long. That's a lot of commitment for one-and-a-half minutes!

You can never knock the feeling of winning – it's a huge boost that makes you want to achieve more. It is an amazing feeling to get your first GB kit.

23

Lifestyle

Gymnasts who are training to succeed at a high level have very little time to themselves. This means that seeing friends and socialising can be difficult to fit in. Most evenings are taken up with training, and weekends are spent catching up with homework or being away at competitions. This can be hard – but these gymnasts are pursuing a dream that will not become a reality without this level of commitment.

Eating to be fit

For any athlete a healthy, balanced diet is essential. Young gymnasts are still growing and must have the correct diet to keep their bodies in good condition. Five portions of fruit and vegetables a day help to provide the required **nutrients** and **minerals**. Along with these, a high **carbohydrate** and low fat intake is necessary to give the body the energy to train well each day.

Money

Gymnasts travel to competitions all over the world. Only a few at the very top level are given help to pay for their travel and accommodation. The rest have to pay for everything themselves. Clubs work hard organising raffles and other activities to raise money to help their gymnasts. Local sponsors can also be a great help.

I eat a healthy, balanced diet. Eating five portions of fruit and vegetables a day is very important to me.

I make sure I eat plenty of carbohydrates, fruit, chicken, eggs and milk. I allow myself treats – but I do watch my weight.

It is recommended that everyone eats at least five portions of fruit and vegetables every day.

Injuries

Gymnasts push their bodies to the limit over and over again, so it is not surprising that they sometimes get injured. Warming up properly before training sessions reduces the risk of pulling muscles, as does the amount of conditioning training that the gymnasts do regularly. Toes can be particularly at risk as gymnasts perform in bare feet or socks.

Safety

Gym clubs work within strict rules to make sure that all the equipment is in good condition and used safely.

A fall from a trampoline can cause serious injury. At gym clubs and in competitions people called 'spotters' are positioned at the side of a trampoline to catch or break the fall of anyone who misjudges a jump. When trampolinists are practising new routines they always have someone on hand to help prevent any mishaps.

School

Fitting in school work can be tricky with the amount of training that gymnasts do. Often the level of discipline that they bring to their training means they are organised in other aspects of their lives, too.

*I was jumping at full height and my ankle rolled over as I landed. I tore four **ligaments** around my ankle and was put in plaster. I couldn't bounce for six weeks – it was awful.*

*I had lots of **physio** and went to the pool to keep my fitness up. It was just before a world trial and I had to go into the trial not having competed for three months. I still qualified.*

It can be difficult to fit everything in sometimes. I do end up doing my school work very late at night. I do well in exams though, so I can't be doing too badly. I don't get much leisure time, but when I do I make the most of it.

I have just started secondary school. I have to fit homework in before and after training.

I have made a great group of friends through the sport. Competitions often finish with a party!

Sporting heroes

Great gymnasts are an inspiration to all those who are training hard to reach the top of their sport.

Fair competition

Gymnasts train very hard to be the best they possibly can. Unfortunately in gymnastics, as in some other sports, there are a few competitors who cheat by using drugs to improve their performance. All drugs that could give a gymnast an unfair advantage are banned. Gymnasts are regularly tested to see if there are any of these illegal drugs in their bodies. A gymnast who is found to have taken illegal drugs risks being banned from the sport.

Kohei Uchimura of Japan, and Great Britain's Daniel Keatings are my favourite gymnasts. They have a neatness and style I admire.

Daniel Keatings
Great Britain
Artistic gymnast
Date of birth: 1 Dec 1990

2009 World Championships – Silver
2008 Junior European Championships – 4 Golds
Junior all-around (on all six pieces of apparatus) Champion

When Daniel Keatings finished in second place in the men's all-around final at the 2009 World Championships he made British history. It was Britain's first all-around medal. He won it in front of a home crowd at the O2 Arena in London.

Daniel Keatings competes on the pommel horse during the men's all-around final at the Artistic Gymnastics World Championships.

I really admire Beth Tweddle. I like the fact that she doesn't give up even though some people think she is too old. At the World Championships in 2009 even though she fell on the bars, she kept her head up and went on to win the floor title.

Beth Tweddle
Great Britain
Artistic gymnast
Date of birth: 1 April 1985

2009 World Championships: Gold (see page 29)
2006 World Championships: Gold
2005 World Championships: Bronze
2003 European Championships: Silver
2003 World Championships: Bronze

Tweddle was the first ever British world champion gymnast when she won the gold medal in asymmetric bars at the 2006 World Championships.

Jason Burnett
Canada
Trampolinist
Date of birth: 16 Dec 1986

2008 Olympic Games: Silver
2007 Pan American Games: Silver
2007 World Cup: Bronze – individual;
Gold – synchronised
2006 Pan American Championships:
Gold

As well as achieving a silver Olympic medal, Burnett is also known for having completed, in training, the world's most difficult trampoline routine.

Jason Burnett and Irina Karavaeva are great trampolinists. They are the best in the world! I like them because they are daring as well as being elegant in the air. I met Jason Burnett in Loule, Portugal, in 2008, after he had broken the world record for the number of twisting doubles in a routine. He was really nice and I now have him as a friend on Facebook!

Sophie with Olympic silver medallist Jason Burnett.

27

The next step

Training to be a top-level competitive gymnast is a long, steady process. The commitment to training will be too much for some and they will leave the sport and pursue other interests. Some will get injured or perhaps realise that they are not talented or committed enough to achieve their goal. Many will remain involved in gymnastics in some other way though, often through training or coaching.

Eyes on the prize

Every gymnast's dream is to win a World Championship, or a gold medal at the Olympic Games.

I am hoping to do a degree in sports studies so when I finish competing I can coach future generations of trampolinists. I would like to work in a role that allows me to develop the sport further in this country.

My next target is to become part of the national squad. Eventually I would like to be number one in the world.

Eventually I would like to go to university and get a degree in Ancient History. But I'll see what opportunities open up for me. If I could go to an American university and continue training, that would be incredible.

In three years time, I would like to be on the British senior team. Then I can start to achieve my overall aim which is to be the European and World Tumbling Champion.

Coach's notes: family

Before we start to put any gymnast through an elite training programme we always sit down and discuss it very carefully with their parents. The level of commitment they will all need is high and it will go on for a long time. They need to be really sure they know what they are letting themselves in for.

Beth Tweddle of Great Britain shows off the gold medal that she won for the floor exercise in the Artistic Gymnastics World Championships, 2009.

Slowly but surely

Miki, Beth, Lucie and Sophie are looking forward to a long and successful career in gymnastics. There is a lot of hard work ahead of them if they are to achieve their dream. Let's wish them all the best of luck.

My ultimate ambition is a medal at the Olympics in 2016 or 2020. Trampolinists tend to be older than other gymnasts. My mum took me to Athens to watch Kirsten Lawton compete for GB in 2004 – it was inspiring.

Glossary

acrobatic gymnastics A type of gymnastics that has acrobatic moves, performed to music.

aerobic gymnastics A type of gymnastics that includes jumps and leaps, performed to music.

apparatus A piece of equipment used in gymnastics competitions.

artistic gymnastics A type of gymnastics in which male gymnasts perform routines on six pieces of apparatus, female gymnasts on four.

asymmetric bars A piece of apparatus used in women's artistic gymnastics. The gymnast swings between a high bar and a low bar.

balance beam A beam five metres long and ten centimetres wide used in women's artistic gymnastics.

carbohydrates A group of foods that includes sugars and starch.

cardiovascular The system that carries blood to and from all parts of the body.

choreography The arrangement and sequence of moves that form a routine.

compulsory Something that has to be done.

conditioning Exercise that improves physical fitness.

contract To become shorter.

core muscles The muscles in the trunk of the body.

cramp A sudden, sometimes painful, contraction of a muscle.

dismount The move used to get off of a piece of apparatus.

double mini-trampoline A specially designed trampoline made in two parts. The gymnast takes a run up and jumps on to the first part of the trampoline, bounces on to the second part then dismounts.

dynamic stretches Stretches done while moving.

elite A group of people who are at the top level in their sport.

handspring A front or back tumbling skill that takes off from the feet, then on to the hands and back on to the feet.

high bar A piece of apparatus used in men's artistic gymnastics. The gymnast performs a routine on a single high bar.

ligament A band of tissue that connects bones.

minerals Elements in food that are essential for our bodies to function correctly.

nutrients The substances in food that are used by the body to grow and stay healthy.

parallel bars A piece of apparatus used in men's artistic gymnastics. The gymnast performs a routine on two bars alongside each other at the same height.

pass A tumbler's routine.

physio (physiotherapy) The treatment of injuries with exercise.

piked A position in gymnastics with the body bent forward from the waist and the legs straight.

plyometrics A type of strength training that helps develop muscle power.

pommel horse A piece of apparatus used in men's artistic gymnastics.

recreational A sport or pastime played or performed for pleasure rather than competition.

rhythmic gymnastics A type of gymnastics in which routines include leaps, turns, balances and flexibility moves while holding a ball, a rope, a hoop, two clubs or a ribbon.

rings A piece of apparatus used in men's artistic gymnastics. The gymnast swings between two rings hanging from the ceiling.

round-off A floor or beam skill similar to a cartwheel, but with both feet landing at the same time.

salto (flip or somersault) An acrobatic move where the gymnast takes off, rotates horizontally, then lands back on the feet.

springboard A flexible board from which a gymnast jumps to take off in tumbling and vaulting.

straddle A position with the body facing forward and the legs stretched out to the side.

static stretches Stretches done while staying still.

synchronise To happen at the same time.

TeamGym A team competition for clubs. The gymnasts have to perform skills in trampette and tumbling as well as a floor exercise. The skills are all done as a team.

trampette A small trampoline.

tuck A body position where the knees are bent and drawn into the chest with the hands holding the knees.

tumble track The 25 m track on which tumblers perform their routine.

tumbling A type of gymnastics in which gymnasts perform a series of somersaults and twists on a 25 m track.

vault A piece of apparatus used in men's and women's artistic gymnastics. The gymnast makes a fast run up to a springboard and then over a vaulting platform, while doing twists and somersaults.

walkover A move used on the beam and in floor exercises.

warm up Gentle exercises to stretch the muscles before more vigorous exercise.

whip A back flip done with the body straight.

Find out more

Websites

http://www.british-gymnastics.org/site/
The official site for gymnastics in Great Britain. It has information on all the different types of gymnastics available in Great Britain. Click on 'WATCH GYMNASTICS TV AND VIDEOS HERE' to find video highlights from recent championships – all types of gymnastics in all age groups.

http://www.welshgymnastics.org
The Welsh Amateur Gymnastics Association official site.

http://www.scottishgymnastics.org/
The Scottish Gymnastics Association official site.

http://www.englishgymnastics.org.uk
The English Gymnastics Association official site.

http://www.irishgymnastics.ie/
The Irish Gymnastics Association official site.

Books

Know Your Sport: Gymnastics (Franklin Watts, 2008)
A guide to gymnastics, with step-by-step photographs as well as profiles and statistics giving information about some of the world's greatest gymnasts.

Know Your Sport: Trampolining (Franklin Watts, 2008)
General information as well as step-by-step photographs showing some basic moves. Profiles and statistics give information about the world's greatest trampolinists.

Note to parents and teachers: every effort has been made by the Publishers to ensure that these websites are suitable for children, that they are of the highest educational value, and that they contain no inappropriate or offensive material. However, because of the nature of the Internet, it is impossible to guarantee that the contents of these sites will not be altered. We strongly advise that Internet access is supervised by a responsible adult.

Index